Melanin Magic
33 Magical Inventors

melaninmagicclub.com

Published By Melanin Magic Club

Melanin Magic Club LTD ©2021

Melanin Magic Club LTD has asserted their moral rights. All rights reserved.

No part of this book may be reproduced in any manner without written permission.

Please visit our website melaninmagicclub.com for books and accessories.

  @MELANINMAGICCLUBUK   @MMCLUBUK

Welcome to 'Atay the Ant's' 33 Magical Melanin Inventors. Atay is one of The Melanin Magic Kids. As a passionate inventor he wanted to teach you about all the wonderful melanated people who have created some of the world's most important inventions. Since the beginning of time melanated people have been inventing and innovating things that have improved the lives of humanity.

Some of the inventors' exact birth dates and the dates of when they died were unknown. Some of these wonderful inventors are still here with us today. Learn about all these magical inventors and be inspired. This could be you, you just need self-belief and focus.

ALFRED L CRALLE
(September 4, 1866 – May 6, 1919)

This is Alfred L Cralle, a black businessman and inventor. He was born in Virginia on September 4th, 1866. He was most famous for inventing the ice cream scoop. He noticed that ice cream servers were finding it difficult to get ice cream into a cone using spoons because the ice cream would stick and they would have to use 2 hands. So he invented the ice cream scoop to make it easier!

Everyone has special gifts and talents, it's what makes us Magical. Search for your gift, and remember, there are no limits to your potential. You could be a successful businessman if you wanted to!

ALICE H PARKER

(1895 – 1920)

This is Alice H Parker, she was born in 1895 in New Jersey. Alice was famous for inventing the heating furnace, she designed the first heating system that was powered by gas.

Everyone has special gifts and talents, it's what makes us Magical. Search for your gift, and remember, there are no limits to your potential. You could be the next famous inventor!

AUGUSTUS JACKSON
(April 16, 1808 – January 11, 1852)

This is Augustus Jackson, he was a top chef from Philadelphia born in 1808. Augustus was famous for his delicious ice cream recipes. He invented a better way of making ice cream that we still use today, it made ice cream taste better.

Everyone has special gifts and talents, it's what makes us Magical. Search for your gift, and remember, there are no limits to your potential. Maybe you're the next famous chef and the inventor of a new recipe?

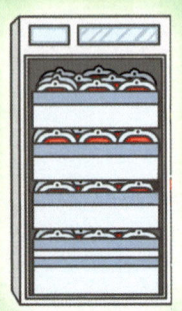 

CHARLES DREW
(June 3, 1904 – April 1, 1950)

This is Charles Drew, he was born in 1904 in Washington. He was an American surgeon and researcher of medicine. He was famous for inventing a way to store and handle blood. He created two of the first blood banks.

Everyone has special gifts and talents, it's what makes us Magical. Search for your gift, and remember, there are no limits to your potential. You could make a big difference in medicine if you wanted to.

DR SHIRLEY ANN JACKSON
(August 5, 1946 -)

This is Dr Shirley Ann Jackson, she was born in 1946 in Washington DC and she is a Theoretical Physicist who is most famous for inventing the technology required for the fax machine, touch-tone phone, fiber optic cells, solar cells and caller ID. Dr Shirley was the first African American woman to earn a doctorate.

Everyone has special gifts and talents, it's what makes us Magical. Search for your gift, and remember, there are no limits to your potential. You could invent a technology that could change the future!

FREDERICK M JONES
(May 17, 1893 – February 21, 1961)

This is Frederick McKinley Jones, he was born in 1893 in Ohio. Frederick was famous for inventing a new way to transport food, blood and medicine by designing the first successful portable air conditioning unit for trucks. This was essential during world war II because food and blood were needed in the battlefields and hospitals.

Everyone has special gifts and talents, it's what makes us Magical. Search for your gift, and remember, there are no limits to your potential. You could be famous for creating a new way to help people all over the world!

GARRETT MORGAN
(March 4, 1877 – July 27, 1963)

This is Garrett Morgan, he was born in 1877 in Paris, Kentucky. Garrett had many inventions including hair care products. However, he was most famous for inventing a new, better traffic light system with three positions. Red, Amber and green, before traffic lights only had "Stop" and "Go". Garrett Morgan added the yellow light which warned drivers to slow down, he made it safer for vehicles to be on the road.

Everyone has special gifts and talents, it's what makes us Magical. Search for your gift, and remember, there are no limits to your potential. You could invent a new way to keep people safe.

GEORGE CRUM

(July 15, 1824 – July 22, 1914)

This is George Crum, he was born in 1824 in New York. He was a chef and was most known for his famous potato chips. George Crum had his own restaurant which served delicious potato chips at every table. George's potato chips were so popular he had wealthy visitors from all over America come to his restaurant to try them.

Everyone has special gifts and talents, it's what makes us Magical. Search for your gift, and remember, there are no limits to your potential. You could be the next chef to create a popular snack that people will love all over the world.

GEORGE WASHINGTON CARVER
(1864 – January 5, 1943)

This is George Washington Carver, he was born in 1864 in Missouri. He was an agricultural scientist and an inventor of many things. George was most famous for creating 300 different uses for peanuts. From peanuts he was able to make milk, cheese, soap, glue and other useful items. He was one of the greatest black inventors in history.

Everyone has special gifts and talents, it's what makes us Magical. Search for your gift, and remember, there are no limits to your potential. You could be a top scientist and inventor too!

GRANVILLE T WOODS
(April 23, 1856 – January 30, 1910)

This is Granville T Woods, he was born in 1856 in Ohio. He had a love for electrics and was the inventor of over 50 electrical products. One of his most exciting and famous inventions was an electric roller coaster called the figure eight.

Everyone has special gifts and talents, it's what makes us Magical. Search for your gift, and remember, there are no limits to your potential. You could be the next maker of an exciting new invention!

HENRY SAMPSON
(April 22, 1934 – June 4, 2015)

This is Henry Sampson, he was born in 1934. He was an engineer and inventor. He was most famous for creating the gamma-electric cell. This invention made it possible to have portable mobile phones. His invention changed the world and how we communicate today.

Everyone has special gifts and talents, it's what makes us Magical. Search for your gift, and remember, there are no limits to your potential. You could be an engineer who designs a new machine that changes the world.

JOHN STANDARD
(June 22, 1868 - 1900)

This is John Standard, he was born in 1868. He was an inventor who was most famous for improving kitchen appliances such as the fridge and the stove. Although he didn't invent the fridge, he invented a new way to improve the design of the fridge. He created a way to have the freezer separate from the main fridge. Many people were impressed with how useful his new fridge invention was. He changed the way people store & cook food.

Everyone has special gifts and talents, it's what makes us Magical. Search for your gift, and remember, there are no limits to your potential. You could be the one that impresses people with your talent!

LEWIS LATIMER

(September 4, 1848 – December 11, 1928)

This is Lewis Latimer, he was born in 1848. He was an inventor who was most famous for inventing the carbon filament, which improved the design of the lightbulb. His new and improved lightbulb lasted longer and was more affordable.

Everyone has special gifts and talents, it's what makes us Magical. Search for your gift, and remember, there are no limits to your potential. You can be the person that improves the way people live.

LISA GELOBTER

(1971 -)

This is Lisa Gelobter, she was born in 1971 and is a computer scientist. She is most famous for being an online animation wizard and creating the animation needed to create GIFS. Lisa has many accomplishments and is one of the most important women in media and technology, her products have been used by billions of people all over the world.

Everyone has special gifts and talents, it's what makes us Magical. Search for your gift, and remember, there are no limits to your potential. You could be the next computer scientist!

LONNIE JOHNSON

(October 6, 1949 -)

This is Lonnie Johnson, he was born in 1949. He is an aerospace engineer and inventor. He invented many different things but is most famous for inventing the super soaker, which was the number one selling toy in the world. He also invented high performance nerf guns.

Everyone has special gifts and talents, it's what makes us Magical. Search for your gift, and remember, there are no limits to your potential. You could create the next toy that children love!

LYDA NEWMAN
(1865 - Unknown)

This is Lyda Newman, she was born in 1865. She was a hairdresser who was most famous for inventing a better hairbrush for people to use. Her hairbrush could be taken apart and cleaned. It was easier to use and stronger.

Everyone has special gifts and talents, it's what makes us Magical. Search for your gift, and remember, there are no limits to your potential. You could be a famous hairdresser who creates new beauty products.

MARIE VAN BRITTAN

(October 30, 1922 – February 2, 1999)

This is Marie Van Brittan, she was born in 1922. She was a nurse and inventor. She was most famous for inventing the world's first home security system. Her invention had peep holes, a camera, microphone, television monitors and an alarm button that could contact the police straight away, she is the reason why we now have CCTV systems that are used everywhere today.

Everyone has special gifts and talents, it's what makes us Magical. Search for your gift, and remember, there are no limits to your potential. You could be the next famous inventor that changes people's lives.

MILDRED DAVISON KENNER　　**MARY DAVISON KENNER**
(January 17, 1916 - 1993)　　　　(May 17, 1912 – January 13, 2006)

This is Mary & Mildred Davidson who are sisters. They were most famous for inventing a sanitary belt, which had a pocket to make it less likely to leak. This invention made it easier for women to be comfortable during their period cycle.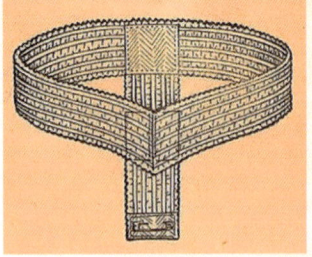

Everyone has special gifts and talents, it's what makes us Magical. Search for your gift, and remember, there are no limits to your potential. You could work with someone as a team to follow your dreams!

PAUL E WILLIAMS
(February 18, 1894 – January 23, 1980)

This is Paul E Willams. He was an architect, he was most famous for developing the first useful helicopter. It was called The Lockheed Model 186 (XH–51).

Everyone has special gifts and talents, it's what makes us Magical. Search for your gift, and remember, there are no limits to your potential. You could be an engineer that develops new technology!

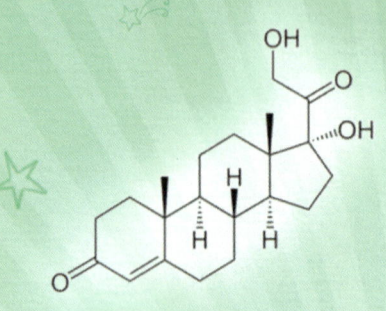 

PERCY JULIAN
(April 11, 1899 – April 19, 1975)

This is Percy Julian, he was born in 1899. He was a research chemist who had over 130 developments in chemistry. He produced the medicine needed to treat arthritis and glaucoma. He also invented Aero–Foam, which is used to put out oil and gas fires. This was very important during World War 2 to extinguish fires and is still made today.

Everyone has special gifts and talents, it's what makes us Magical. Search for your gift, and remember, there are no limits to your potential. You could produce a medicine that makes people better!

PHILIP EMEAGWALI
(August 23, 1954 -)

This is Philip Emeagwali, he was born in 1954. He is a computer scientist. He is most famous for inventing the world's fastest computer, some people called it the super computer! He changed the internet completely by programming wires and computers that had record breaking speeds.

Everyone has special gifts and talents, it's what makes us Magical. Search for your gift, and remember, there are no limits to your potential. You could solve problems using technology!

RICHARD SPIKES

(October 2, 1878 - January 22, 1963)

This is Richard Spikes, he was born in 1878. He was an inventor who had a love for mechanics. He had many inventions but was most famous for inventing an automatic gear shift device for cars.

Everyone has special gifts and talents, it's what makes us Magical. Search for your gift, and remember, there are no limits to your potential. You could work as an engineer and design new products for cars!

SARAH BOONE
(February 1832–1904)

This is Sarah Boone, she was born in 1892. She was a dressmaker and inventor. She was most famous for inventing a modern– day ironing board. Before her invention people were ironing their clothes using a wooden plank, which wasn't suitable. Sarah created a board that was easier to use, could fold up and down and was better at ironing clothes, especially sleeves and ladies' clothes.

Everyone has special gifts and talents, it's what makes us Magical. Search for your gift, and remember, there are no limits to your potential. You could invent household goods that change the way people use things!

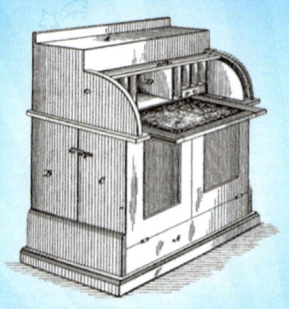

SARAH GOODE

(1855 – April 8, 1905)

This is Sarah Goode, she was born in 1885. She owned a furniture shop and was most famous for inventing a folding bed that was able to fit into small homes. She wanted to help people who lived in small homes and didn't have much space. It was a bed that folded into a desk.

Everyone has special gifts and talents, it's what makes us Magical. Search for your gift, and remember, there are no limits to your potential. You can be a successful entrepreneur and own shops too.

THOMAS ELKINS
(1818 – August 10, 1900)

This is Thomas Elkins, he was born in 1818. He was a dentist, surgeon, pharmacist and inventor. He invented lots of different things. One of them was an improved modern day toilet. It had a mirror, table, wash stand and rack.

Everyone has special gifts and talents, it's what makes us Magical. Search for your gift, and remember, there are no limits to your potential. You could use your skills to develop new products!

BENJAMIN MONTGOMERY
(January 25, 1858 – Unknown)

This is Benjamin Montgomery he was born into slavery in 1819. He was a skilled mechanic and inventor. Benjamin had great techniques for flood control. At the time, trade goods traveled throughout rivers across different states and counties however, the different depths of water made navigation difficult. If a boat went adrift it could delay delivery for weeks. Benjamin changed this by creating a propeller that could cut into the water at different angles, this allowed boats to navigate easier through shallow water.

Everyone has special gifts and talents, it's what makes us Magical. Search for your gift, and remember, there are no limits to your potential. You could also create new techniques that help make things easier.

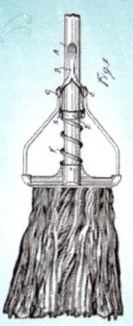 

THOMAS W STEWART
(1823 – Unknown)

This is Thomas Stewart. He was an inventor most famous for creating a new and better mop. His mop had clamps and springs so you could wring out the water when you used it, which made cleaning easier. He also made the mop head come apart so it was easier to clean.

Everyone has special gifts and talents, it's what makes us Magical. Search for your gift, and remember, there are no limits to your potential. You could be the next person to create something that makes people's everyday lives easier!

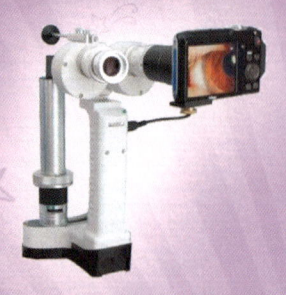
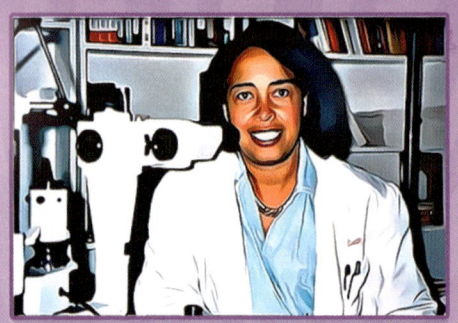

PATRICIA E BATH

(November 4, 1942 – May 30, 2019)

This is Patricia Era Bath, she was an American ophthalmologist, inventor, humanitarian, and academic. She was the inventor of laser cataract surgery for the eyes. Her invention was called Laserphaco Probe. Amongst several other firsts, Bath was the first African-American woman doctor to receive a patent for a medical purpose.

Everyone has special gifts and talents, it's what makes us Magical. Search for your gift, and remember, there are no limits to your potential. You could also dedicate your time to helping heal others.

LEONARD C BAILEY
(1825 - September 1, 1918)

This is Leonard C. Bailey, he was an black entrepreneur, inventor, and banker. He founded one of the first African–American banks in the United States. Bailey invented and received patents for a series of devices, many designed for military and government use. One of these inventions included the folding bed.

Everyone has special gifts and talents, it's what makes us Magical. Search for your gift, and remember, there are no limits to your potential. You could also change the world with your inventions.

GERALD LAWSON
(December 1, 1940 – April 9, 2011)

This is Gerald Lawson, he was an American electronic engineer. He is known for his work in designing the Fairchild Channel F video game console, it was the first console that had video game cartridges. An innovation that is still relevant to this day.

Everyone has special gifts and talents, it's what makes us Magical. Search for your gift, and remember, there are no limits to your potential. You could also make big developments in the gaming industry!

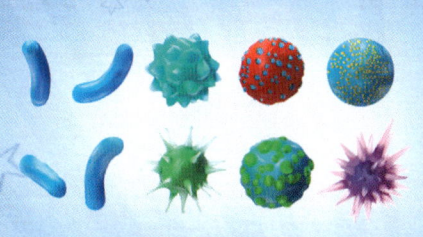 

EMMETT CHAPPELLE
(October 24, 1925 – October 14, 2019)

This is Emmett W. Chappelle, he was an American scientist. He was one of the greatest modern day scientists and engineers who won many awards. He discovered lots of important findings in Biology and Chemistry. He discovered new ways in which scientists can detect and measure bacteria in outer space. He also discovered that single-cell organisms can convert carbon dioxide into sugar and water into oxygen.

Everyone has special gifts and talents, it's what makes us Magical. Search for your gift, and remember, there are no limits to your potential. You could also make huge developments within science.

VALERIE THOMAS

(February 8, 1943)

This is Valerie L Thomas, she is an American scientist and inventor who has a love for technology, maths and science. She is most famous for inventing the illusion transmitter and for all her contributions to NASA research. She also made real-time computer data systems to support satellite operations and control centers.

Everyone has special gifts and talents, it's what makes us Magical. Search for your gift, and remember, there are no limits to your potential. You could also make developments in the way we see and capture images.

Printed in Great Britain
by Amazon